YE·LIBRARIE OF

Sarah V. Clement

Poetry

COLLECTED POEMS OF *Elinor Wylie*

SELECTED POEMS *Witter Bynner*

IDEAS OF ORDER *Wallace Stevens*

APRIL TWILIGHTS *Willa Cather*

THE COLLECTED POEMS OF *Stephen Crane*

THE COLLECTED VERSE OF *Robert Hillyer*

These are BORZOI BOOKS, *published by*
ALFRED A. KNOPF

MORE POEMS

A. E. Housman, July 1926,
from a drawing by Francis Todd

A. E. Housman

MORE POEMS

ALFRED A. KNOPF

NEW YORK

1936

PREFACE

This final selection of A. E. Housman's poems
is published by his permission, not by his wish.
His instructions, allowing them to appear, while
committing other material to a less fortunate
fate, were as follows:

" I direct my brother, Laurence Housman, to
destroy all my prose manuscripts in whatever
language, and I permit him but do not enjoin him
to select from my verse manuscript writing, and
to publish, any poems which appear to him to be
completed and to be not inferior to the average
of my published poems; and I direct him to destroy all other poems and fragments of verse."

The responsibility which has thus been laid on
me is of a double character; for while I am anx-
ious to include nothing that can do hurt to my
brother's literary reputation, I am most reluctant
to deprive his lovers of any poems, however

v

minor in character, which are not inferior to others — also minor in character — which have already been published.

So far as he himself was concerned, he had no desire to add to the two selections he had already made, either from the poems then left out, or from the few which were written subsequently. But consideration for the wishes of others became increasingly apparent in his last years; and since he has made me the instrument of that consideration, I feel bound to give it as sympathetic an interpretation as possible.

My main difficulty has been this: that while I would naturally wish to give any poem of minor merit the benefit of the doubt, and am therefore inclined to err on the side of leniency, I know well that his own decision would be more likely to err on the side of severity. But since in only one case has he crossed out a finished poem with the written comment "not good," it would seem that he intended to leave all the rest freely to my own judgment — average merit and completeness being the limiting conditions.

Several of these poems, as were some of *Last Poems* also, are of *Shropshire Lad* date, and though the name of *Terence* does not reappear, it is evident that a good many, especially those from page 20 to page 44 belong to the *Terence* series, and, through the mouth of that imaginary character, express, sometimes contradictorily, the turbulent and changing moods of troubled youth. In an autobiographical note supplied to a French writer, " The Shropshire Lad," my brother explained, " is an imaginary character, with something of my temper and view of life. Very little in the book is biographical."

In the present volume only the poem bearing initials for title, and one or two toward the end are directly personal. The earlier group above referred to are poems of a time of life which the author had long passed when he wrote them; but none the less they are characteristic of the lively sympathy which, in the words of the opening poem of this collection, he had for all ill-treated fellows, and more especially for the young. He would have liked " the laws of God and man " to be kinder than they are; and a great deal of the anger and bitterness of his verse is due to the fact that they are so much the other way.

Several of these poems were paged and numbered for inclusion in *Last Poems*, and one of them (No. XLV) was actually printed; but as the author had previously left out from *A Shropshire Lad* verses which appeared later in *Last Poems*, I do not take omission to mean final rejection.

The poem " For my funeral " was written in 1925, and was, as shown in the list of dated poems, given at the end of this volume, the last to have its date recorded. Only the poems named in this list have been dated by the author; but from their place of sequence in a set of four closely-filled notebooks, the dates of a good many other poems can be inferred. These notebooks I am under orders to destroy; but before doing so I intend to make a paged list of their contents which will give a fairly accurate chronology of most of the published poems.

It may be some consolation for those who regret this order for destruction, to know that there are no fragments or unfinished poems of outstanding quality. A few beautiful phrases, sometimes single verses, will have to go. One or two which, in spite of extreme brevity, seemed to stand on their own I have felt justified in retaining. All the rest is mainly work-shop material — chiefly of interest as showing the author's method of composition — his many alterations of phrase or rhyme before finding the one which best satisfied him. I am fortunately able, however, to give one example of alternative readings — a poem (No. X) of which there existed two complete variants, with no indication as to which of the two the author preferred; and though I have a slight preference myself, I am not so confident of my judgment being right as to deny to others the interest and pleasure of making their own choice.

In choosing between other variant readings limited to single lines, words, or phrases, and also in making the selection which here follows, I have been greatly helped by the kind services and wise counsel of three of my brother's colleagues of Trinity. Professor G. M. Trevelyan, O.M., Mr. Andrew Gow, and Mr. F. L. Lucas; and though they are not to be held finally responsible for what has here been included, and what left out, their good advice — for which I am most grateful, has had a not inconsiderable influence on the selection as it now stands.

I have also to thank the President and Fellows of St. John's College, Oxford, for their kind per-

mission to reproduce the Francis Dodd drawing
which forms the frontispiece, and which in my
view is the best portrait of my brother that has
ever been done.

L. H.

CONTENTS

xiii

MORE POEMS

They say my verse is sad: no wonder;
  Its narrow measure spans
Tears of eternity, and sorrow,
  Not mine, but man's.

This is for all ill-treated fellows
  Unborn and unbegot,
For them to read when they're in trouble
  And I am not.

3

I

EASTER HYMN

If in that Syrian garden, ages slain,
You sleep, and know not you are dead in vain,
Nor even in dreams behold how dark and bright
Ascends in smoke and fire by day and night
The hate you died to quench and could but fan,
Sleep well and see no morning, son of man.

But if, the grave rent and the stone rolled by,
At the right hand of majesty on high
You sit, and sitting so remember yet
Your tears, your agony and bloody sweat,
Your cross and passion and the life you gave,
Bow hither out of heaven and see and save.

II

When Israel out of Egypt came,
 Safe in the sea they trod;
By day in cloud, by night in flame,
 Went on before them God.

He brought them with a stretched-out hand
 Dry-footed through the foam,
Past sword and famine, rock and sand,
 Lust and rebellion, home.

I never over Horeb heard
 The blast of advent blow;
No fire-faced prophet brought me word
 Which way behoved me go.

5

Ascended is the cloudy flame,
 The mount of thunder dumb;
The tokens that to Israel came,
 To me they have not come.

I see the country far away
 Where I shall never stand;
The heart goes where no footstep may
 Into the promised land.

The realm I look upon and die
 Another man will own;
He shall attain the heaven that I
 Perish and have not known.

But I will go where they are hid
 That never were begot,
To my inheritance amid
 The nation that is not.

Where mixed with me the sandstorms drift,
   And nerve and heart and brain
Are ashes for the air to lift,
   And lightly shower again.

III

For these of old the trader
  Unpearled the Indian seas,
The nations of the nadir
  Were diamondless for these;

A people prone and haggard
  Beheld their lightnings hurled:
All round, like Sinai, staggered
  The sceptre-shaken world.

But now their coins are tarnished,
  Their towers decayed away,
Their kingdom swept and garnished
  For haler kings than they;

Their arms the rust hath eaten,
    Their statutes none regard:
Arabia shall not sweeten
    Their dust with all her nard.

They cease from long vexation,
    Their nights, their days are done,
The pale, the perished nation
    That never see the sun.

From the old deep-dusted annals
    The years erase their tale,
And round them race the channels
    That take no second sail.

IV

THE SAGE TO THE YOUNG MAN

O youth whose heart is right,
  Whose loins are girt to gain
The hell-defended height
  Where virtue beckons plain;

Who seest the stark array
  And hast not stayed to count
But singly wilt assay
  The many-cannoned mount:

Well is thy war begun;
  Endure, be strong and strive;
But think not, O my son,
  To save thy soul alive.

10

Wilt thou be true and just
  And clean and kind and brave?
Well; but for all thou dost
  Be sure it shall not save.

Thou, when the night falls deep,
  Thou, though the mount be won,
High heart, thou shalt but sleep
  The sleep denied to none.

Others, or ever thou,
  To scale those heights were sworn;
And some achieved, but now
  They never see the morn.

How shouldst thou keep the prize?
  Thou wast not born for aye.
Content thee if thine eyes
  Behold it in thy day.

O youth that wilt attain,
　On, for thine hour is short.
It may be thou shalt gain
　The hell-defended fort.

V

The snows are fled away, leaves on the shaws
  And grasses in the mead renew their birth,
The river to the river-bed withdraws,
  And altered is the fashion of the earth.

The Nymphs and Graces three put off their fear
  And unapparelled in the woodland play.
The swift hour and the brief prime of the year
  Say to the soul, *Thou wast not born for aye.*

Thaw follows frost; hard on the heel of spring
  Treads summer sure to die, for hard on hers
Comes autumn with his apples scattering;
  Then back to wintertide, when nothing stirs.

13

But oh, whate'er the sky-led seasons mar,
 Moon upon moon rebuilds it with her beams;
Come *we* where Tullus and where Ancus are
 And good Aeneas, we are dust and dreams.

Torquatus, if the gods in heaven shall add
 The morrow to the day, what tongue has told?
Feast then thy heart, for what thy heart has had
 The fingers of no heir will ever hold.

When thou descendest once the shades among,
 The stern assize and equal judgment o'er,
Not thy long lineage nor thy golden tongue,
 No, nor thy righteousness, shall friend thee
 more.

Night holds Hippolytus the pure of stain,
 Diana steads him nothing, he must stay;
And Theseus leaves Pirithous in the chain
 The love of comrades cannot take away.

VI

I to my perils
   Of cheat and charmer
   Came clad in armour
   By stars benign;
Hope lies to mortals
   And most believe her,
   But man's deceiver
   Was never mine.

The thoughts of others
   Were light and fleeting,
   Of lovers' meeting
   Or luck or fame;

Mine were of trouble
And mine were steady,
So I was ready
When trouble came.

VII

Stars, I have seen them fall,
　But when they drop and die
No star is lost at all
　From all the star-sown sky.
The toil of all that be
　Helps not the primal fault;
It rains into the sea
　And still the sea is salt.

VIII

Give me a land of boughs in leaf,
  A land of trees that stand.
Where trees are fallen, there is grief;
  I love no leafless land.

Alas, the country whence I fare,
  It is where I would stay,
And where I would not, it is there
  That I shall be for aye.

And one remembers and forgets
  But 'tis not found again,
Not though they hale in crimsoned nets
  The sunset from the main.

IX

When green buds hang in the elm like dust
　And sprinkle the lime like rain,
Forth I wander, forth I must,
　And drink of life again.

Forth I must by hedgerow bowers
　To look at the leaves uncurled,
And stand in fields where cuckoo flowers
　Are lying about the world.

X

The weeping Pleiads wester
  And the moon is under seas;
From bourn to bourn of midnight
  Far sighs the rainy breeze:

It sighs from a lost country
  To a land I have not known;
The weeping Pleiads wester,
  And I lie down alone.

XI

The rainy Pleiads wester,
  Orion plunges prone,
And midnight strikes and hastens,
  And I lie down alone.

The rainy Pleiads wester
  And seek beyond the sea
The head that I shall dream of
  That will not dream of me.

XII

I promise nothing: friends will part;
　All things may end, for all began;
And truth and singleness of heart
　Are mortal even as is man.

But this unlucky love should last
　When answered passions thin to air;
Eternal fate so deep has cast
　Its sure foundation of despair.

XIII

I lay me down and slumber,
  And every morn revive.
Whose is the night-long breathing
  That keeps me man alive.

When I was off to dreamland
  And left my limbs forgot,
Who stayed at home to mind them,
  And breathed when I did not?

I waste my time in talking,
  No heed at all takes he,
My kind and foolish comrade
  That breathes all night for me.

23

XIV

The farms of home lie lost in even,
  I see far off the steeple stand;
West and away from here to heaven
  Still is the land.

There if I go no girl will greet me,
  No comrade hollo from the hill,
No dog run down the yard to meet me:
  The land is still.

The land is still by farm and steeple,
  And still for me the land may stay:
There I was friends with perished people,
  And there lie they.

24

Tarry, delight, so seldom met,
  So sure to perish, tarry still;
Forbear to cease or languish yet,
  Though soon you must and will.

By Sestos town, in Hero's tower,
  On Hero's heart Leander lies;
The signal torch has burned its hour
  And sputters as it dies.

Beneath him, in the nighted firth,
  Between two continents complain
The seas he swam from earth to earth
  And he must swim again.

XV

Tarry, delight, so seldom met,
 So sure to perish, tarry still;
Forbear to cease or languish yet,
 Though soon you must and will.

By Sestos town, in Hero's tower,
 On Hero's heart Leander lies;
The signal torch has burned its hour
 And sputters as it dies.

Beneath him, in the nighted firth,
 Between two continents complain
The seas he swam from earth to earth
 And he must swim again.

XVI

How clear, how lovely bright
How beautiful to sight
  Those beams of morning play;
How heaven laughs out with glee
Where, like a bird set free,
Up from the eastern sea
  Soars the delightful day.

To-day I shall be strong,
No more shall yield to wrong,
  Shall squander life no more;
Days lost, I know not how,
I shall retrieve them now;
Now I shall keep the vow
  I never kept before.

* * *

Ensanguining the skies
How heavily it dies
   Into the west away;
Past touch and sight and sound
Not further to be found
How hopeless underground
   Falls the remorseful day.

XVII

Bells in tower at evening toll,
And the light forsakes the soul;
Soon will evening's self be gone
And the whispering night come on.

Blame not thou the faulting light
Nor the whisper of the night;
Though the whispering night were still,
Yet the heart would counsel ill.

XVIII

Delight it is in youth and May
    To see the morn arise,
And more delight to look all day
    A lover in the eyes.
Oh, maiden, let your distaff be,
And pace the flowery meads with me,
    And I will tell you lies.

'Tis blithe to see the sunshine fail,
    And hear the land grow still,
And listen till the nightingale
    Is heard beneath the hill.
Oh, follow me where she is flown
Into the leafy woods alone,
    And I will work you ill.

XIX

The mill-stream, now that noises cease,
Is all that does not hold its peace;
Under the bridge it murmurs by,
And here are night and hell and I.

Who made the world I cannot tell;
'Tis made, and here am I in hell.
My hand, though now my knuckles bleed,
I never soiled with such a deed.

And so, no doubt, in time gone by,
Some have suffered more than I,
Who only spend the night alone
And strike my fist upon the stone.

XX

Like mine, the veins of these that slumber
  Leapt once with dancing fires divine;
The blood of all their noteless number
  Ran red like mine.

How still, with every pulse in station,
  Frost in the founts that used to leap,
The put-to-death, the perished nation
  How sound they sleep!

These too, these veins which life convulses,
  Wait but a while, shall cease to bound;
I with the ice in all my pulses
  Shall sleep as sound.

XXI

The world goes none the lamer
    For aught that I can see,
Because this cursed trouble
    Has struck my days and me.

The stars of heaven are steady,
    The founded hills remain,
Though I to earth and darkness
    Return in blood and pain.

Farewell to all belongings
    I won or bought or stole;
Farewell, my lusty carcase,
    Farewell, my aery soul.

Oh worse remains for others,
And worse to fear had I
Than here at four-and-twenty
To lay me down and die.

XXII

Ho, everyone that thirsteth
　And hath the price to give,
Come to the stolen waters,
　Drink and your soul shall live.

Come to the stolen waters
　And leap the guarded pale,
And pull the flower in season
　Before desire shall fail.

It shall not last for ever,
　No more than earth and skies;
But he that drinks in season
　Shall live before he dies.

34

June suns, you cannot store them
To warm the winter's cold,
The lad that hopes for heaven
Shall fill his mouth with mould.

XXIII

Crossing alone the nighted ferry
  With the one coin for fee,
Whom, on the wharf of Lethe waiting,
  Count you to find? Not me.

The brisk fond lackey to fetch and carry,
  The true, sick-hearted slave,
Expect him not in the just city
  And free land of the grave.

XXIV

Stone, steel, dominions pass,
    Faith too, no wonder.
So leave alone the grass
    That I am under.
All knots that lovers tie
    Are tied to sever;
Here shall your sweetheart lie,
    Untrue for ever.

XXV

Yon fire that frets the eastern sky
    Leads back my day of birth;
The far wide-wandered hour when I
    Came crying upon earth.

Then came I crying, and to-day,
    With heavier cause to plain,
Depart I into death away,
    Not to be born again.

XXVI

Good creatures, do you love your lives
    And have you ears for sense?
Here is a knife like other knives,
    That cost me eighteen pence.

I need but stick it in my heart.
    And down will come the sky,
And earth's foundations will depart
    And all you folk will die.

XXVII

To stand up straight and tread the turning mill,
To lie flat and know nothing and be still,
  Are the two trades of man; and which is worse
I know not, but I know that both are ill.

XXVIII

He, standing hushed, a pace or two apart,
  Among the bluebells of the listless plain,
Thinks, and remembers how he cleansed his heart
  And washed his hands in innocence in vain.

XXIX

From the wash the laundress sends
My collars home with ravelled ends;
I must fit, now these are frayed,
My neck with new ones London-made.

Homespun collars, homespun hearts,
Wear to rags in foreign parts.
Mine at least's as good as done,
And I must get a London one.

XXX

Shake hands, we shall never be friends, all's over,
   I only vex you the more I try;
All's wrong that ever I've done or said,
And naught to help it in this dull head;
   Shake hands, here's luck, good-bye.

But if you come to a road where danger
   Or guilt or anguish or shame's to share
Be good to the lad that loves you true
And the soul that was born to die for you,
   And whistle and I'll be there.

XXXI

Because I liked you better
   Than suits a man to say,
It irked you, and I promised
   To throw the thought away.

To put the world between us
   We parted, stiff and dry;
" Good-bye," said you, " forget me."
   " I will, no fear," said I.

If here, where clover whitens
   The dead man's knoll, you pass,
And no tall flower to meet you
   Starts in the trefoiled grass,

44

Halt by the headstone naming
The heart no longer stirred,
And say the lad that loved you
Was one that kept his word.

XXXII

With seed the sowers scatter
  The furrows as they go.
Poor lads, 'tis little matter
  How many sorts they sow,
  For only one will grow.

The charlock on the fallow
  Will take the traveller's eyes,
And gild the ploughland sallow
  With flowers before it dies,
  But twice 'twill not arise.

The stinging nettle only
  Will still be found to stand:

The numberless, the lonely,
   The thronger of the land,
   The leaf that hurts the hand.

It thrives, come sun, come showers;
   Blow east, blow west, it springs;
It peoples towns, and towers
   Above the courts of Kings;
   And touch it and it stings.

XXXIII

On forelands high in heaven,
  'Tis many a year gone by,
Amidst the fall of even
  Would stand my friends and I.
Before our foolish faces
  Lay lands we did not see;
Our eyes were in the places
  Where we shall never be.

Oh, the pearl seas are yonder,
  The gold and amber shore;
Shires where the girls are fonder,
  Towns where the pots hold more.
And here fret we and moulder

By grange and rick and shed,
And every moon are older,
  And soon we shall be dead.

Heigho, 'twas true and pity;
  But there we lads must stay.
Troy was a steepled city,
  But Troy was far away.
And round we turned lamenting
  To homes we longed to leave,
And silent hills indenting
  The orange band of eve.

I see the air benighted
  And all the dusking dales,
And lamps in England lighted,
  And evening wrecked in Wales;
And starry darkness paces
  The road from sea to sea,
And blots the foolish faces
  Of my poor friends and me.

XXXIV

Young is the blood that yonder
　　Strides out the dusty mile,
And breasts the hillside highway
　　And whistles loud the while,
　　And vaults the stile.

On miry meads in winter
　　The footballs sprung and fell;
May stuck the land with wickets:
　　For all the eye could tell,
　　The world went well.

Yet well, God knows, it went not,
　　God knows it went awry;

For me, one flowery Maytime,
    It went so ill that I
    Designed to die.

That passed; and long I carry
    The life that season marred,
Because the child of Adam
    Is not so evil-starred
    As he is hard.

Yet flesh, now too, has thorn-pricks,
    And shoulders carry care,
Even as in other seasons,
    When I and not my heir
    Was young and there.

Young is the blood that yonder
    Succeeds to rick and fold,
Fresh are the form and favour,
    And new the minted mould:
    The thoughts are old.

XXXV

Half-way, for one commandment broken,
  The woman made her endless halt;
And she to-day, a glittering token,
  Stands in the wilderness of salt.
Behind, the vats of judgment brewing
  Thundered, and thick the brimstone snowed;
He to the hill of his undoing
  Pursued his road.

XXXVI

Here dead lie we because we did not choose
    To live and shame the land from which we
        sprung.
Life, to be sure, is nothing much to lose;
    But young men think it is, and we were young.

XXXVII

I did not lose my heart in summer's even
    When roses to the moonrise burst apart:
When plumes were under heel and lead was
    flying,
    In blood and smoke and flame I lost my heart.

I lost it to a soldier and a foeman,
    A chap that did not kill me, but he tried;
That took the sabre straight and took it striking,
    And laughed and kissed his hand to me and
    died.

XXXVIII

By shores and woods and steeples
   Rejoicing hearts receive
Poured on a hundred peoples
   The far-shed alms of eve.

Her hands are filled with slumber
   For world-wide labourers worn;
Yet those are more in number
   That know her not from morn.

Now who sees night for ever,
   He sees no happier sight:
Night and no moon and never
   A star upon the night.

XXXIX

My dreams are of a field afar
  And blood and smoke and shot.
There in their graves my comrades are,
  In my grave I am not.

I too was taught the trade of man
  And spelt the lesson plain;
But they, when I forgot and ran,
  Remembered and remain.

XL

Farewell to a name and a number,
 Recalled again
To darkness and silence and slumber
 In blood and pain.

So ceases and turns to the thing
 He was born to be
A soldier cheap to the King
 And dear to me.

So smothers in blood the burning
 And flaming flight
Of valour and truth, returning
 To dust and night.

57

XLI

He looked at me with eyes I thought
    I was not like to find;
The voice he begged for pence with brought
    Another man to mind.

Oh, no, lad, never touch your cap;
    It is not my half-crown:
You have it from a better chap
    That long ago lay down.

Turn east and over Thames to Kent
    And come to the sea's brim,
And find his everlasting tent
    And touch your cap to him.

XLII

A. J. J.

When he's returned I'll tell him — oh,
 Dear fellow, I forgot:
Time was you would have cared to know,
 But now it matters not.

I mourn you, and you heed not how;
 Unsaid the word must stay;
Last month was time enough, but now
 The news must keep for aye.

Oh, many a month before I learn
 Will find me starting still,
And listening, as the days return,
 For him that never will.

59

Strange, strange to think his blood is cold
    And mine flows easy on;
And that straight look, that heart of gold,
    That grace, that manhood gone.

The word unsaid will stay unsaid
    Though there was much to say;
Last month was time enough: he's dead,
    The news must keep for aye.

XLIII

I wake from dreams and turning
    My vision on the height
I scan the beacons burning
    About the fields of night.

Each in its steadfast station
    In flaming heaven they flare;
They sign with conflagration
    The empty moors of air.

The signal fires of warning
    They blaze, but none regard,
And on from night to morning
    The world runs ruinward.

61

XLIV

Far known to sea and shore,
   Foursquare and founded well,
A thousand years it bore,
   And then the belfry fell.
      The steersman of Triest
         Looked where his mark should be;
      But empty was the west
      And Venice under sea.

From dusty wreck dispersed
   Its stature mounts amain;
On surer foot than first
   The belfry stands again.
      At to-fall of the day

Again its curfew tolls,
And burdens far away
    The green and sanguine shoals.

It looks to north and south,
    It looks to east and west;
It guides to Lido mouth
    The steersman of Triest.
        Andrea, fare you well;
            Venice, farewell to thee.
        The tower that stood and fell
            Is not rebuilt in me.

XLV

Smooth between sea and land
Is laid the yellow sand,
And here through summer days
The seed of Adam plays.

Here the child comes to found
His unremaining mound,
And the grown lad to score
Two names upon the shore.

Here, on the level sand,
Between the sea and land,
What shall I build or write
Against the fall of night?

Tell me of runes to grave
That hold the bursting wave,
Or bastions to design
For longer date than mine.

Shall it be Troy or Rome
I fence against the foam,
Or my own name, to stay
When I depart for aye?

Nothing: too near at hand,
Planing the figured sand,
Effacing clean and fast
Cities not built to last
And charms devised in vain,
Pours the confounding main.

XLVI

THE LAND OF BISCAY

Sons of landsmen, sons of seamen, hear the tale
of grief and me,
Looking from the land of Biscay on the waters
of the sea.

Looking from the land of Biscay over Ocean to
the sky
On the far-beholding foreland paced at even
grief and I.
There, as warm the west was burning and the
east uncoloured cold,
Down the waterway of sunset drove to shore a
ship of gold.

Gold of mast and gold of cordage, gold of sail
   to sight was she,
And she glassed her ensign golden in the waters
   of the sea.

Oh, said I, my friend and lover, take we now
   that ship and sail
Outward in the ebb of hues and steer upon the
   sunset trail;
Leave the night to fall behind us and the clouding
   countries leave:
Help for you and me is yonder, in the havens
   west of eve.

Under hill she neared the harbour, till the gazer
   could behold
On the golden deck the steersman standing at
   the helm of gold,
Man and ship and sky and water burning in a
   single flame;

And the mariner of Ocean he was calling as he
    came:
From the highway of the sunset he was shouting
    on the sea,
" Landsman of the land of Biscay, have you help
    for grief and me? "

When I heard I did not answer, I stood mute and
    shook my head:
Son of earth and son of Ocean, much we thought
    and nothing said.
Grief and I abode the nightfall; to the sunset
    grief and he
Turned them from the land of Biscay on the
    waters of the sea.

XLVII

O thou that from thy mansion
  Through time and place to roam,
Dost send abroad thy children,
  And then dost call them home,

That men and tribes and nations
  And all thy hand hath made
May shelter them from sunshine
  In thine eternal shade:

We now to peace and darkness
  And earth and thee restore
Thy creature that thou madest
  And wilt cast forth no more.

XLVIII

ALTA QUIES

Good night. Ensured release,
Imperishable peace,
  Have these for yours.
While sky and sea and land
And earth's foundations stand
  And heaven endures.

When earth's foundations flee,
Nor sky nor land nor sea
  At all is found,
Content you; let them burn,
It is not your concern:
  Sleep on, sleep sound.

XVII, line 2, *for* light *read* day

line 5, *for* faulting *read* blinded

XXXIV, *for stanza four read*

And if so long I carry

The lot that season marred,

'Tis that the sons of Adam

Are not so evil-starred

As they are hard.

DATED POEMS

The following are the poems to which dates are given in the Author's note-books. All but two were published either in *A Shropshire Lad* or in *Last Poems*.

ONCE IN THE WIND OF MORNING	Sept.	1890
IN SUMMER-TIME ON BREDON	July	1891
FAR IN A WESTERN BROOKLAND		1891–2
'TIS TIME, I THINK, BY WEN- LOCK TOWN	Feb.	1893
THE WEEPING PLEIADS WESTER	Feb.	1893
FAREWELL TO BARN AND STACK AND TREE	Aug.	1894
THE LAD CAME TO THE DOOR AT NIGHT	Dec.	1894
WHEN I WAS ONE-AND-TWENTY	Jan.	1895
WAKE: THE SILVER DUSK RE- TURNING	Jan.	1895
LEAVE YOUR HOME BEHIND, LAD	Jan.	1895
HIGH THE VANES OF SHREWS- BURY GLEAM	Jan.	1895

ON MOONLIT HEATH AND LONE-SOME BANK	Feb.	1895
FAR I HEAR THE BUGLE BLOW	March	1895
'TIS SPRING: COME OUT TO RAM-BLE	April	1895
OH, WHEN I WAS IN LOVE WITH YOU	May	1895
ALONG THE FIELD AS WE CAME BY	June	(1895?)
WHEN I CAME LAST TO LUDLOW	July	1895
HERE THE HANGMAN STOPS HIS CART	Aug.	1895
MORNING UP THE EASTERN STAIR	Sept.	1895
IN MY OWN SHIRE, IF I WERE SAD	Nov.	1895
YONDER SEE THE MORNING BLINK	Dec.	1895
THE CHESTNUT CARTS HIS FLAMBEAUX	Feb.	1896
WAKE NOT FOR THE WORLD-HEARD THUNDER	30 March	1922
ONWARD LED THE ROAD AGAIN	10 April	1922
O THOU THAT FROM THY MAN-SION		1925

73

THIS BOOK *was composed by The Plimpton Press,*
Norwood, Massachusetts. It was printed and
bound by The Haddon Craftsmen, Camden,
New Jersey. The paper was made by P. H. Glat-
felter Co., Spring Grove, Pa. The typography
and design are by W. A. Dwiggins.